Jeremy, Interrupted

Jeremy, Interrupted

True Stories About a
Learning Disabled Boy

Jeremy Mutzabaugh

TREMENDOUS
LEADERSHIP
Leadership with a kick!

JEREMY, INTERRUPTED

True Stories About a Learning Disabled Boy

Published by:
Tremendous Leadership
PO Box 267
Boiling Springs, PA 17007
717-701-8159 800-233-2665

www.TremendousLeadership.com

ISBN: 978-1-947033-06-9

Printed in the United States of America.

DEDICATION

I've written this book to give encouragement to students who struggle in school with learning difficulties. Those who run into problems with teachers or classmates can find hope in the fact that they can get through the school years and thrive. I've had several years of challenges with classmates and teachers because of a disability.

I pushed myself through my school years—not focusing on what others thought or said. I chose to look at the silver linings in the dark clouds that seemed to hang above me and focused on a brighter future after my education was complete. Here is a glimpse of what my schooling was like and some of the hardships I walked through.

Jeremy Mutzabaugh

TABLE OF CONTENTS

FOREWORD

When I received the query from Jeremy about his desire to publish a book, I knew I was in for a tremendous blessing. Our first meeting revealed a future author full of experiences, and challenges turned into opportunities, ready to be poured out. Jeremy's ability to reflect on his life and to give thanks for everything that transpired showed me that this was an incredibly unique individual with a story that needed to get out there.

Jeremy's story is one of triumph, not tragedy. His thick skin, tender heart, open mind, and faith in God is a testimony that all things do work together for good to those that love the Lord and are called unto his purpose (Romans 8:28). This book is to encourage anyone who has doubted themselves because of teachers, classmates, or toxic personalities in the workplace. You'll walk away with a renewed self-confidence and ability to diminish the biting words of your critics. When you have a dream in your heart, follow it; don't follow your peers because that will lead to mediocrity.

Jeremy not only shares how he did it but how we can do it as well. Don't let any disabilities, real or perceived, stop you from unceasingly blessing the world.

Tracey C. Jones
President
Tremendous Leadership

Chapter One

ELEMENTARY SCHOOL

I was put into Special Education in my first year of Elementary School. Compared to other students, it always took me longer to learn new things.

In kindergarten, my teacher wanted us to draw a picture of the home we resided in. I almost failed because I drew what was obviously a double-wide trailer. At the time, this was what my family and I lived in. After the assignments were turned in, the teacher thought I was playing a game and called my folks in for a meeting.

Throughout my schooling, my parents worked as a comfort/support team for me at home. They never gave up on me and always believed in me. When they met with my teacher, they told her that what I had drawn was correct—it was where we lived—much to her embarrassment.

* * * *

I remember timed Math tests each week when I was in the first, second, and third grades. We were given copies of Math problems, and we had three minutes to answer as many as we could. I always dreaded these because they were given under a time frame and Math was my worst subject. The stress of taking timed tests compounded my great dislike for the topic. But eventually, with much studying, I overcame this.

* * * *

I also had subjects like Art, Music, and Physical Education. Each spring our class would meet at an athletic field with Special

Education students from other schools in the district. Here we would compete in the areas of track and field, throwing a disc through the air, throwing softballs for length, and running up to a sandbox and jumping for a measured distance.

This was great fun for everyone who participated. I really enjoyed the freedom of playing and running without the fear of being made fun of, or compared to others of similar age who had more athletic prowess.

* * * *

Some years our teachers would buy the *Weekly Reader* magazine. The class would have to take turns reading an article from it. *Weekly Reader* always had a write-up about current events. I remember some of the topics we learned about were on farming, and another time it was about NASA. The articles were always interesting, and each week there was something new to read about.

The magazine would sometimes have order forms to purchase books. I bought books from the school this way. We had the option to fill out the form, enclose a check, turn it in, and the school would send the order in for you.

Ordering books was a great memory during this time. I always looked forward to getting something new to read in the mail.

Chapter Two

JUNIOR HIGH

The atmosphere was different in seventh grade, and it took some getting used to. Adjusting to the many different personalities of the students and teachers was only one of the many challenges that I had.

I had to become familiar with sprinting from one classroom to the next—in between—stopping at my locker for the different books used for each topic. Then there were my classmates and their incessant whining about *everything*. These were only some of the problems I had to deal with. Needless to say, my Junior High days were rough, but I continued to push through.

* * * *

There was one ray of hope during my journey through these years. I had a teacher that was good at teaching, and this quickly won my respect and admiration. He was an assistant coach to our football team. One day he asked me to come on board and join them as a manager. I thought my heart would burst. I'll never forget his kindness and being open-minded enough to give me a chance.

* * * *

My classmates and I were always called "speds" by the other students. For some reason, they thought they were better than us. This attitude stuck us with a bullseye on our backs and no one to defend us.

An extreme example of this occurred while attending a Physical Education (PE) session. I developed an extreme hatred for this class. In order to pass, I had to strip naked and shower with the other boys from my Special Education class. Some of them were quite vicious. They took great pleasure in using towels to snap at us when we were naked—laughing at us and mocking us as we cried out in pain—yet the teacher would do nothing about it.

* * * *

Our Physical Education teachers were also our Health class instructors. On one occasion, we were waiting for our teacher to arrive so our Health class could start. He was late showing up. When he finally came, the class was talking very loudly and really carrying on. He couldn't get them to calm down and suddenly became furious. He screamed at everyone in the room, "Everyone sit down! I'm not in the mood to be here today and teach you! I didn't want to teach you in the first place! You are all a bunch of speds and retards!"

The next day, all the students were called in to talk with the principal. The reason for this was that several classmates had told their parents about the incident and their parents, in turn, called the school. The teacher ended up being reprimanded.

We found out later what had happened before our Health class. Right before our Health Instructor came to teach us, he had taught a Gym class. During this class, there was an accident where one of the students injured themselves very badly. An ambulance needed to be called to take the injured student to the hospital. When the teacher came to our class, he was still upset about the injury, and the trauma the student suffered. Our class, with its raucous behavior, had set him over the edge.

While this explains his reaction towards us, it still did not excuse his behavior, and it was good that he was reprimanded.

* * * *

Another time while attending Junior High, I was getting books out of my locker when a classmate bumped into me from behind and removed my wallet from a back pocket. He had pickpocketed me! It happened so fast I only had a moment to recognize who it was before he slipped away through a crowd of students.

In a way, I wasn't too upset because there was only five cents in my wallet at the time. During my next class, I was called to the principal's office. As I stepped into the room, I saw the boy who had lifted my wallet and couldn't help but notice that he was holding it wrapped in a paper towel.

While the principal stood beside him, the boy told me he had just found the wallet in a urinal in the men's room—but I knew different. He had run down the hall with the wallet, hoping to steal some cash. When he got to the bathroom, he threw the wallet into the urinal, pulled it out, and took it to the office with his fabricated lie.

I never attempted to refute what he said because I knew that it would have made my life even more difficult by placing us at odds with each other. Besides, I could get a new wallet, and he didn't get any of my money.

* * * *

The only person out of all the teachers and students from my Junior High years that I kept in touch with was the teacher that I admired. Sad to say, he has since passed on. I have lost contact with everyone else. I moved on to the next grade never giving a thought to my former harassers.

Chapter Three

SENIOR HIGH

I went to Vocational Technical School in Senior High. By the time I was in eleventh and twelfth grade, I was taking all mainstream classes. These included the topics: Related Drawing, Economics, Computer Literature, Biology, English Literature, Business Law, and Family Living.

In every term, I made the honor roll throughout my high school years. I made Distinguished Honors—that is an "A" in every class—once in twelfth grade. In my shop class, I was elected Safety Foreman. Having this position meant that I was responsible for keeping the shop in a safe learning atmosphere. My duties included making sure all the tools were put away at the end of the day, keeping cords and plugs working right—making sure they were not broken, keeping the floors clean and dry, and replacing burned out light bulbs.

When I graduated I ranked 18th out of 188 graduates. Not bad for someone who had started out in Special Education. I was proud of my accomplishments and all that I had achieved despite my disability and the negativity from teachers and students along the way.

****

I did go to my high school prom, but for most of the year, I wasn't sure if I would go. I was shy, and I think every guy knows how hard it is to ask a girl out. I finally got the nerve and asked a nice ninth grade girl to go with me. I was surprised when she said, "Yes."

I remember when we walked into the hotel where the dance was held—I could feel everyone staring at us. After dinner, my date went to the bathroom and came back with her hair dropped down out of the veil she previously had it tucked into. She looked even more beautiful. When she came back to the table, I knew people were really looking at us.

The next week at school I had a female classmate harass me. She said, "Jeremy, I didn't expect you to go to the prom, never mind bringing a date. I didn't even know who she was until she came back to the table. What is your problem, Jeremy? She's a ninth grader!" I calmly stated, "She is our classmate, she goes to this school, there is nothing wrong with what I did." She said, "That is not the point," implying the age difference between us made it wrong.

I'm glad I spoke my mind to her. Sometimes people build false cases against you in their minds based on their opinion.

I've learned that it's important for your self-esteem to speak up and tell the truth on your behalf.

Chapter Four

COLLEGE YEARS

I choose to go to college for two years. My folks were promised I would be put in classes with instructors who knew how to teach learning disabled students. This turned out to not be true.

My first term, I had an English professor who showed an outright hatred for me from day one. For every paper I turned in to him he would hand it back with "See Me" scrawled at the top. Every time I went to his office, he wouldn't want to help me. As soon as I arrived at his office door, he would say, "Go to the tutoring center, that's what they are there for."

My tutor at the center finally asked me who my instructor was. When I said the man's name, she told me, "I'm sorry, I can't help you. I had to drop his class last year." This confirmed to me what a difficult class and difficult person this was. I knew my odds of earning a passing grade were very low. By this time I was holding a solid "F" in the class. I had just enough time left in the semester to transfer out of this class and finish the term with a different instructor, with a "C" as my ending grade.

Here my persistence paid off. I knew I wasn't a "sped" and wanted to learn. From my previous years of education, I learned to push through to reach my goals—even though other people don't encourage you to do so.

* * * *

I had some roommates in college that liked to play games. I shared a small, two-story apartment with seven other boys. One evening as I was walking back from class, I saw a police car, two policemen, and a tow truck parked outside our apartment building. The driver of the tow truck had it backed up to my car which was pushed out into the street and was hooking chains to my vehicle.

I approached the officers. The one asked, "Is this your car?" I said, "Yes, what's going on?" The policeman asked, "Why is it parked in the street?" I said, "Sir, I just walked back from class and I'm not sure what's going on." He said, "Is this a joke?" "No." I replied. "I had it parked here, on the cement," pointing to the appropriate parking space where it should have been. He looked me squarely in the eyes and asked, "Does someone else have a key to it?" "No...my roommates must be playing games," I said as I thought out loud. "Well, park it out of the way and if it was your roommates and they don't settle down, call us." He made this remark in a loud, distinct voice looking towards the open windows of the apartment.

After the tow truck and police left, I moved my car back to where it should have been. Walking through the front door, I wasn't surprised to see my roommates all waiting for me. Everyone was feigning innocence and saying things like, "Did you see that car parked out there? We didn't know whose it was. We called to have it towed." The smirks on their faces and stifled laughter gave them away. "No kidding, it was *my* car," was my only reply as I walked upstairs to my room.

I knew I didn't have to say anything else because the windows were open and they had heard what the policeman had said... "if it was your roommates and they don't settle down, call us." Needless to say, there were no more games played at my expense.

* * * *

The boy I shared the bedroom with brought a girl home one night. I had no idea what I was about to walk into.

After coming back from an evening class, I entered the apartment and noticed how quiet it was. It seemed as if no one was home. I went upstairs and saw that our bedroom door was closed. I gently turned the knob and slowly pushed the door open thinking my roommate might be taking a nap.

Opening the door, I saw that it was quite the contrary. Having never seen anything like it before, I stared for a moment as I watched a tangle of naked flesh engaged in what was obviously sexual activity.

I casually walked over to my side of the room and put my books down—ignoring the motions and moans coming from behind me. I started to gather some clean clothes from my drawer to get ready to take a shower.

They finished their act. The girl quickly got dressed and left. As soon as the door closed behind her, my roommate unleashed his fury on me, shouting, "Next time knock before you enter my room!" I replied, "This was my room long before it was yours. I will not knock to enter my room." He gathered his things and moved to the back bedroom.

It was a good experience for me—although vulgar in some aspects. Here I learned to stand up for my rights and boldly speak up for myself without fear.

* * * *

The most exciting time I had while living with my seven roommates happened on a Wednesday night. All the boys from the first floor went to a party down the street.

It was midnight before they came home, and I knew this because I woke up from a sound sleep hearing their loud laughter and the slamming of doors. They were all very drunk. Everyone upstairs was in bed.

No one knew this at the time, but one of the boys who was out partying had a shotgun under his bed. For some reason—most likely because of his level of intoxication—he decided to take the gun out.

Putting a bullet into the chamber of the gun, he fired a round off in his bedroom. Luckily, he had the gun pointed ahead of him. Our rooms were only separated by one piece of plywood, so the bullet traveled through the wall of the living room coming out the other side. If he would have pointed up, he may have killed me, seeing that my bedroom was right over his.

We all ran to his room at the sound of the gunshot. It was amazing to see how the other inebriated boys sobered up at the sound of a gun going off. We opened the door of his room to see him passed out on his bed holding his weapon—which we immediately removed and stored in a safer place.

Seeing the poor choice in his inebriated condition encouraged me in the future to never drink to excess, if at all.

* * * *

One of my favorite memories while attending college was when the school booked Holly Dunn to come and give a concert. Holly sang country music—and boy could she ever. My personal opinion is that this was when country music was still understandable and people knew how to sing.

While attending the concert, she walked off stage in the middle of one of her songs. Coming down the stairs, she moved along the wall on one side of the room. As she passed the seated section in front of the stage, she came up into the bleachers near where I was sitting. I could hardly believe she was standing so close to me. She finished her song and cracked some jokes with the people sitting behind me. She looked to her side, then down and saw me looking up at her. I raised my hand, and we shook hands, then she walked down and back to the stage.

It was a time I will never forget—one that I will always cherish. It's beautiful moments like these that are the ones to remember as we journey through this life.

* * * *

During my time at college, out of all the professors that I had to teach me, I only had respect for two of my forestry instructors. Maybe this was because they respected me, and treated me kindly—giving me their time when I asked for help. They are both retired now, and I think of them fondly when they come to mind.

After graduating from college, I've only kept in touch with one of my classmates over the years. I know many people don't keep connections with people from their past, but I believe it's essential, if you can, to maintain relationships with people that have walked with you through good and bad times.

Chapter Five

EXCURSIONS

Several years after college, I went to a bluegrass concert. I had never been to a bluegrass show and really wanted to go, so I went to the show by myself. A few minutes after the band started playing, a beautiful woman walked in and sat at a table in the middle of the building. I couldn't help but notice that she was alone. I walked up to an empty seat beside her and through the evening, asked her a couple questions. We talked randomly throughout the night. As the concert ended and people were leaving, I asked, "Would you like to go out and see a movie sometime?"

She hesitated before she answered and said, "No, I better not. I'm on the outskirts of a rocky relationship right now."

Although I wish things would have turned out differently, I was glad she was honest. I haven't crossed paths with her since—but I still remember her—she was stunning. Again, though nothing transpired, I was proud of myself for having the courage to sit near her, carry on a conversation, and ask her out. It was a great morale booster for me.

* * * *

I took a bus tour to Baltimore one day, to the National Aquarium. After receiving the tour, our group waited for the bus to return and pick us up. While waiting, I sat on a park bench by myself and watched the people and traffic go by. Suddenly, out of nowhere, a woman ran up to me shouting, "Sir! Sir! Could you help me? I need a little money to get home. I have no money, and the bus fare is $2.00." I was startled at how a woman who had never met me before could walk up to me (a complete stranger) and ask for money. Looking her over—she seemed like an honest person—I gave her five dollars. She said, "Thank you!" and hugged me. I asked her where her home was and she pointed over in a nearby direction.

I didn't question things at that time, but a few years later while traveling on a different bus, I asked the driver about this area of Baltimore. I was told there was a homeless shelter near the Aquarium and if someone left the shelter in the morning, they would have to be back by a particular time in the evening, or they could never come back. I thought that was odd to do to a person who had no home, but knew it was probably to deter drug or alcohol use and keep people off the streets at night.

Looking back, I'm still confident in the decision I made at that moment. Although I didn't have a lot of information about the woman or her situation, I trusted a gut feeling that she was sincere and I'm glad I did. I've found that sometimes we need to make decisions not based on what we see, but what we hear on the inside.

* * * *

In December of 2003, I went on a cruise. This was something I had always wanted to do, so I took the step and made the reservation. I flew into Fort Lauderdale, Florida and boarded the ship there. We left port on a Sunday evening. Our first stop was at Nassau in the Bahamas, then to Road Town on the island of Tortola. After Tortola, we went on to Philipsburg on the island of St. Maarten, back to the Bahamas to Half Moon Cay, then finally ending back where we started in Fort Lauderdale, Florida.

I didn't know what to expect since this was my first cruise. There were well over two thousand people on board. The name of the ship was the MS Westerdam. It had a big movie theater, a stage for live performances, a library, wine shop, several stores, a pool deck with a hydro pool and swimming pool, cafes, two restaurants and a nightclub with an in-house DJ. One of the most fun times I had was meeting a famous celebrity and his family.

Overall, I had a wonderful time experiencing new things and meeting new people on this cruise. What I garnered from the trip is that life is so much more interesting if you step outside of your everyday routine or comfort zone. Your journey here can be a great adventure...if you make it that way.

Conclusion

BE ENCOURAGED

I have found several Bible verses that have given me comfort throughout my struggles:

Ecclesiastes 3:1-2, 7 tells me:

"To everything, there is a season, and a time to every purpose under the heaven: A time to be born, and a time to die... a time to keep silence, and a time to speak."

Lamentations 3:22-23:

"It is of the LORD's mercies that we are not consumed, because his compassions

fail not. They are new every morning: great is thy faithfulness."

Ephesians 5:15-16 (NIV):

"Be very careful, then, how you live—not as unwise but as wise, making the most of every opportunity, because the days are evil."

You have to believe in yourself, even if it seems like no one wants to help you. You cannot control other people's actions or attitudes, all you can do is bear with other people, study hard, push yourself and follow your dreams. Make friends with your classmates and if you can't—as a last resort—keep to yourself if you feel you cannot trust anyone and mind your own business. If something does not involve you, don't make it your business. I have come to a really peaceful place in my life. Now, I can usually let things go. Things that used to bother me before do not bother me now. I have stopped trying to control circumstances I have no control over. If my life were to end soon, I would have lived a satisfied, fulfilled life. Life is an awesome gift from God, and I do try to rejoice every day—just as Psalm 118:24 tells us:

> *"This is the day which the LORD hath made; we will rejoice and be glad in it."*

I have learned to count each day as another day to embrace. I wake up each morning, and I'm glad I have another day of life because tomorrow is not promised to me. When I can, I ask for forgiveness for the mistakes I've made and try not to worry about the past. I don't like complaining about yesterday. I love the time I have now, and when I think of tomorrow, I think of all the enjoyable things that may happen. I also try to not waste time with people who are cynical about life and do nothing but complain. These people usually do not know what they are talking about or are stuck in a rut of "stinkin' thinkin'"—as Charlie "Tremendous" Jones used to say.

My time and life are too precious, and life is too short to waste. When I think about the good times I've had in life, or the beautiful blessings God has given me—this is where I find the most happiness. I walk away from any evil thoughts or memories except for remembering how God brought me through them. I know if I focus on all life's disappointments it will only lead to depression. I rejoice in good health and think about my good memories and how much God has blessed me. I try to make my present better by celebrating today and redeeming the time I have left by living the life God gave me to the fullest.

ABOUT THE AUTHOR

Jeremy Mutzabaugh is a native of Central Pennsylvania whose training is in Forestry, Conservation, and Ornamental Horticulture. He has also taken classes at the Citizen's Police Academy through a local police department. Jeremy works doing manual labor and has a passion for serving and helping others. He enjoys the mountains, horses, and meeting new people.

YES, YOU CAN WRITE IN THIS BOOK

YES, YOU CAN WRITE IN THIS BOOK